DON'T UPSE'

CW01669355

An out-sized Suffolk Punch horse

See page 62

DON'T UPSET THE CHOIR

By

REG FRARY

With Illustrations by

IAN M. GOLDIE

NORHEIMSUND BOOKS AND CARDS
1, Whitney Road,
Burton Latimer,
Kettering
Northamptonshire
NN15 5SL

DON'T UPSET THE CHOIR was first published by A.R. Mowbray & Co. Ltd in 1962. Republished by Norheimsund Books and Cards in 1991.

Cover illustration by
Madeleine R. Parker.

© Reg. Frary 1991

By the same author

DON'T BLAME THE ORGANIST
NEVER MIND THE VICAR
LAUGHTER IN CHURCH
ANCIENT AND MODERN
WHAT ABOUT THE CHOIR, VICAR?

ISBN 0 948852 26 7

Printed by Peter Dawes Printers
6 Canon Street, Kettering, Northamptonshire
Tel: (0536) 85524.

FOREWORD

WAS there anywhere in England a church choir which satisfied the whole congregation and the parson?

As a chorister of long standing I doubted it, but the idea to investigate was a fascinating one.

During holidays I have taken many opportunities of singing in church choirs all over England, and I've had some fantastic experiences.

REG FRARY

TO MY FRIEND JOHN SNOW, WHO FIRST SUGGESTED THAT I SHOULD WRITE THE AWFUL TRUTH ABOUT CHURCH CHOIRS

DON'T UPSET THE CHOIR

THE INVISIBLE GENIUS

ONE of my most unbelievable experiences was during a visit to a church deep in the border country of Monmouthshire a few years ago. It was a very old and very big church, lighted by gas-lamps which were switched on by electricity. As soon as I noticed this I thought that here was no ordinary set-up. And it wasn't!

Having been invited to join the choir for my one Sunday's stay in the town, I arrived good and early for Matins.

The entrance to the vestry involved one little step up, followed immediately by another little step down. This was a special device designed to hurtle the unwary visitor head-first into the place, thereby affording some harmless amusement for the choirboys.

But there were no choirboys in the vestry just then. Two men sat on a form, under a clock with no hands. One was the local undertaker, and was very jolly: rising, he shook my hand, said he was a bass, and seemed to be measuring me up with a professional eye.

The other man, whom I can only call the Ancient One, didn't attempt to raise himself, or even his eyes, but grated at me, 'Tenor or bass?' When I replied that I was an alto he looked either shocked or disgusted, but I couldn't quite make out which because his face was almost hidden in the *News of the World*.

Just then a large woman of uncertain age lightly negotiated the trick steps. She was a contralto, I learned. (It's funny how so many contraltos are large women of uncertain age.) She was very businesslike, and asked me what I was. Presuming she referred to my voice, I said 'Alto,' whereupon she, like the Ancient One, appeared shocked or disgusted and took no more notice of me.

It was now fully 10.35, and as the service was supposed to start at 10.30, the choir began to arrive in earnest. Everybody soon managed to find his or her robes, on somebody else's peg or on the floor, and all twenty of us were ready in a big huddle at the chancel door when the Vicar ambled in to start proceedings.

Suddenly a loud gurgling noise filled the vestry, and an attractive soprano, noticing the consternation on my face, explained, 'It's the water—it blows the organ.' She was right, no doubt, but it sounded to me more like blowing a hurricane.

Anyway, the organist played so loudly as we processed in that all other sounds were lost; so that was all right.

When he had subsided, and we were safely installed in the chancel, the undertaker, who had started to suck a peppermint, slid a pile of books along the stall to me—a veteran *English Hymnal*, an *A. & M.* with no cover, an *Old Cathedral Psalter* which fully lived up to its name, and an early number of *Schoolgirls' Own*.

The Vicar announced the first hymn, 'Through the night of doubt and sorrow,' and the organist broke forth joyously again at breakneck speed, before anyone had found the place.

A splendidly unconventional character was this man. Apparently he had nothing whatever to do with the choir, and worked quite independently. Either they had upset him a long time ago, and he had given them up as a bad job, or he had just grown forgetful. I was told later that only the oldest members even remembered what he looked like, for he hadn't peeped round the curtain in the organ-loft for years.

We all finished the hymn round about the same time, and things went quite smoothly until we reached the *Benedictus*. Then I became completely fogged. The undertaking bass kindly pointed out the chant to me, and the organist kindly played an entirely different one. In the manner of basses, the undertaker bawled on regardlessly, but the attractive soprano, who knew about blowing organs with water, turned round and said that the organist *did* sometimes change the chants, and that the one he was now playing wasn't in the book.

I thanked her very much, and had quite an enjoyable time making up my own harmony, but it couldn't have been anything like the harmony which the contralto was making up, because she glared across the chancel at me and tried to bawl even louder than the undertaker—a wild impossibility.

By this time the choirboys had settled down to their own devices, kneeling devoutly and reading their comics under the book-rests. The rest of us were still quite keen, however, but there seemed to be a little misunderstanding about the responses. The invisible genius in the organ-loft apparently decided that contrary to custom they should be sung unaccompanied. This manoeuvre *did* catch everyone on the wrong foot, and so the first three responses were both unaccompanied and unsung.

But we rallied splendidly in the singing of the next hymn. It was something deep and obscure from the *English Hymnal*, and went to a tune on a separate manuscript which someone had forgotten to give out.

Undaunted, some tenors opposite me rendered the whole thing in a high unison so heartily that we all joined in—even the boys.

The acoustics of the church must have been a trifle defective, because from the choir stalls it was quite impossible to hear what the Vicar was saying in the sermon. And it wasn't the fault of any noise in the choir, because all the boys and even some of the women were very quiet, reading their comics, and most of the men had settled down for a nap.

I couldn't get interested in my copy of *Schoolgirls' Own*, and found a fascination in surreptitiously watching the congregation who apparently *could* hear the sermon.

They were all awake, and I think some were finding the next hymn which they had no intention of singing. The others looked grateful for a sit-down, and were quite happy.

We finished strongly with 'Glorious things of Thee are spoken,' and the organist was so carried away by Haydn's famous tune that he played an extra verse. We all acted quickly, however, and sang the last verse over again—all except the attractive soprano in front of me. She sang the first verse again.

We processed out in a very attractive shambles, the boys and women neck and neck in front, and the bass undertaker bringing up the rear in his most professional manner.

The town outside was completely dead at this hour, so most of the adult members made their way to the Conservative Club for a drink, and the boys started a fight in the graveyard.

It wasn't the fault of any noise in the choir

As I left, the Ancient One, still clutching the *News of the World*, told me aggressively that I'd have to go a long way to meet up with another choir like theirs. I agreed.

CABBAGES AND THINGS

I TOOK another opportunity of singing in a different church choir when I visited a relative in a small Suffolk market town a year ago. My relative is himself a member of the choir and is, roughly speaking, a bass.

On our way to Matins on Sunday morning he explained that owing to the clergy shortage the parishes of St. Mary's and Holy Trinity had recently been merged under one rector, and the choirs of the two churches combined to sing morning services at St. Mary's and the evening services at Holy Trinity.

The organist of Holy Trinity was a very advanced and clever young man, and because he was so advanced and clever he realized that any hymn tune which was popular with the congregation must naturally be in the worst possible taste and therefore should be suppressed. Indeed he had told the rector who appointed him that he would never, but *never*, pander to morons who wallowed in debased sentimentality.

The organist of St. Mary's, on the other hand, *always* pandered to morons who wallowed in debased sentimentality. Consequently the morons, thus splendidly catered for, always sang jubilantly and enthusiastically, and were quite undeterred by the Holy Trinity organist who dismissed their efforts as brute force and ignorance.

On this particular Sunday morning Harvest Festival was being celebrated at St. Mary's, and when we arrived the church was crammed with fruit, vegetables and people.

Many of the people were there for the first time since Christmas to make sure that their fruit and vegetables had been placed in the most prominent positions.

The whole display was arranged in a highly original manner, and at the back of the church, round the entrance to the choir vestry it looked as though a laden Covent Garden market lorry had overturned.

Inside the vestry the Holy Trinity organist was suffering. He always suffered on Sunday mornings when he came to St. Mary's because he had to take his place in the choir and process up the church through what he shudderingly described as a mass of people bawling their heads off, completely out of tune with the organ which was out of tune anyway.

I was well received, but no one seemed to have heard of an alto before, and I don't think they quite knew what to do with me. Eventually, however, they put me at the top end of one of the choir stalls between the principal soprano and a malformed marrow.

It appeared that everybody in both choirs had made a special effort to be present for the Harvest Festival, and the St. Mary's organist really beamed with pleasure through the bunches of carrots which festooned his console as he watched us crushing ourselves into the stalls and pushing potatoes backwards and forwards along the book-rests to make room for our music.

My recollections of the service can best be described in those classic words, beloved of all who write reports on choir and Sunday school outings for parish magazines—a good time was had by all. Or all but one in this case.

We seemed to be continuously singing hymns from huge *A. & M.* books which had been presented to the choir by a local post office official and were rubber stamped on almost every page, 'St. Mary's Church, not to be taken away.' No one ever trusts church choristers.

My relative who sings, roughly speaking, bass, sang it very roughly that morning and, with the rest of us, was most exhilarated with the whole proceedings.

The organist of St. Mary's

Even the Holy Trinity organist sang the last hymn with a slightly relaxed expression on his face, but, as the principal soprano told me afterwards, that was only because he was looking forward to Evensong at his own church, and was happy with the thought that he'd found a new tune for 'Come, ye thankful people, come,' which the congregation couldn't possibly sing or even want to sing.

The St. Mary's organist really excelled himself with the voluntary after the service, and very nearly succeeded in drowning the din from the choir vestry as members disrobed and stood about in each other's way making polite conversation. From the vestry we joined the main stream of the congregation trying to leave by the main door of the church.

Even this presented a problem, however, because some choirmen who were market gardeners were involved in a heated discussion over the rival merits of some particularly bloated cabbages in the porch.

It was only when they spotted the St. Mary's organist, with whom they had discussed the Sunday morning service at 'The Three Loggerheads' every Sunday for the last thirty years, that they gave over and allowed the flood through.

The principal soprano joined my relative and me, and said she hoped I would be in the choir at Holy Trinity for Evensong.

She was a delightful girl with a delightful smile, so, readily overlooking the very advanced and very clever young organist who never pandered to morons and who had a new tune for 'Come, ye thankful people, come,' I braced myself and assured her I'd face it!

THE OASIS AND THE WILDERNESS

FOLLOWING my usual practice of endeavouring to sing in the local church choir whenever I am on holiday, I called one evening some years ago on the rector of a small Wiltshire village.

The Rectory was a delightful Regency building, almost hidden behind walls which would have done justice to a prison.

Once inside the gates, the front garden was a joy to behold. There was nothing formal about it. It was really a back-to-nature effort, and consisted mainly of vast numbers of uninhibited hollyhocks interspersed with hordes of unchecked dandelions which were much bigger and more flamboyant than any I had ever dug out of the lawn at home.

The lawn in this case was unique and full of character, wandering all over the paths and half way up the front steps. And gracing the whole scene, adding that indefinable old-world touch, there stood in the centre of the lawn a twenty-ton traction engine.

The rector, opening the door and noting the admiration on my face, explained eagerly that he was the chairman of the local traction engine society which held those breathtaking, exciting races over ploughed fields every bank holiday.

I said I was grateful that at least *some* people were saving the steam-engine from extinction, and, beaming, he led me into a large kitchen-like apartment with a stone-flagged floor.

As it was a rather chilly evening, he drew up a settle in front of a magnificent black and brass range which stretched along one entire wall.

The rector, a middle-aged unobtrusive type, was apparently a bachelor, and pointed out that notwithstanding its beauties the house was perhaps just a little inconvenient for him, having twelve bedrooms, no bathrooms, no domestic staff, and the aforementioned range which burned about half a ton of coal a day and provided stone-cold water in every part of the house at all times.

No one lived with him, but in the cathedral-like stables at the rear of the rectory he nurtured a gigantic Shire horse who kept winning prizes at agricultural shows—and never did any work at all. He did, however, obviate the necessity of mowing the lawn.

The rector, who admitted that he was completely fascinated by Shire horses and traction engines, started to expand on the subjects, and as I also admire those symbols of massive power we should have gone on till midnight had I not suddenly recalled the purpose of my visit.

As I mentioned the choir, the rector's whole being seemed to change, and he became as a broken man. Shuddering as he forced a haggard smile, he stammered: 'Yes, we have a very good choir here—very enthusiastic—perhaps just a *little*—er—*overwhelming* at times.'

'Overwhelming?' I queried, and he explained.

The choir was really a kind of union, he said, and its members formed large majorities on the parochial church council and all the other committees in the parish. Consequently the choir ran the whole church. '—But a good bunch,' he ended dutifully. 'A good bunch.'

I was now very eager to meet this bunch, so the rector took me along to Evensong and left me in the choir vestry

That indefinable old-world touch

till some members should arrive. Two gentlemen soon appeared, and as they saw me one politely inquired of the other in a fascinating brogue: 'What's 'e want?'

I was indeed impressed by the open-hearted welcome.

After staring at me as if I were something from outer space, they shook hands with paralysingly friendly grasps. Even when they learned that I was an alto they intimated very clearly that they didn't hold that against me: after all, I couldn't help it. I felt really at home. . . .

Just before 6.30, when Evensong was due to commence, a little man who bore a striking resemblance to Napoleon Bonaparte suddenly called a meeting of the choir in a dark corner of a vestry.

Apparently someone had suggested removing the gravestones in the churchyard, and he wanted to know what everybody thought about this, so that they could all think the same and solidly oppose the idea at the forthcoming church council meeting.

They all thought the same very quickly, and that problem being disposed of, there appeared to be just one other question to settle.

This entailed gathering round a hymn book with much head-shaking. Then Napoleon went over to the rector and told him that the choir could not do as he had mildly suggested and sing the first hymn to the second tune because they had *always* sung the first hymn to the *first* tune.

The rector said he quite understood, and we all processed into the chancel.

The church was lighted by oil-lamps on ornate brass standards. They shed a gentle, soothing light, and the heat was terrific.

To give them their due, the choir were first rate, and there was no doubt that the organist was a great improvement on his predecessor, a lady who had played the same two chants for the *Magnificat* and the *Nunc Dimittis* for thirty-five years. I began to enjoy myself immensely.

A little overwhelming at times

It was when we reached the anthem that we ran into the only little squall in the whole service.

Goss's 'The Wilderness' was to be sung, and the bass soloist was Napoleon. Just as the rector made the announcement Napoleon's lamp went out, and a kindly disposed man next to me quickly passed down his own lamp to take its place.

It was the worst thing he could have done. Evidently Napoleon interpreted the action as a suggestion that he couldn't sing the famous recitative without consulting the music, because half way through the chorus I found the lamp thrust back into my hands, causing me to miss my place and nearly ruin the whole thing.

After the service the rector invited the choir to the rectory for a cup of tea. They thanked him and said they'd be along later. A meeting had been called to discuss Napoleon's faulty oil-lamp. . . .

NO VACANCIES

A HOLIDAY in a small village on the North Devon Coast provided me with yet another fascinating experience of singing in a church choir other than my own.

The vicar, who said that if I really *wanted* to sing in the choir I was very welcome—and made it sound like a desperate warning—took me along to the church before Evensong to show me some of its finer features.

Certainly the exterior would have presented the most pleasing proportions, had it not been for an expansive parish councillor who at some time had had a family mausoleum built on to it for himself. It was nearly as big as the chancel.

Inside, the church was crammed in all directions with the tombs of the local landed gentry, from Norman times to the end of the eighteenth century. After that period no one had had any chance of interment there as all the best places had been taken, and it would have necessitated removing the pulpit and remaining pews to get them in.

From the inscriptions, which not only covered the tombs but also the entire walls and most of the floor, it appeared that the departed ones had all been pious, charitable, peerless examples of Christian Saints. Historical records which I consulted later, however, proved that most of them had been experts in licentiousness, hard drinking, highway robbery and discreet murder. And at least one highly respected eighteenth-century churchwarden had worked up a profitable little business in the smuggling line.

The villagers had never condemned this behaviour on the part of their betters, but had in fact proudly defended it as being in the great British tradition of adventure and freedom.

The vicar, as he conducted me round, and under and over the tombs, made it quite clear that the two real villains in the history of the Church of England were Oliver Cromwell and James Wyatt the architect. This particular church had suffered from the attentions of them both.

Cromwell was deeply suspicious of everyone connected with the place, and as soon as he got the chance had sent some men along with big hammers to knock the noses and ears off the tomb effigies so that they resembled not so much peerless saints as broken-down boxers. And later Wyatt had dealt an equally unforgivable blow to two of the largest and most hideous tombs in the church.

Under the guise of restoration he had demolished a wall against which the monstrosities were built, and had left them lying around, like discarded packing cases, in a dark corner which eventually turned itself into the lumber room. This lumber room was also the choir vestry.

The vicar never entered it, and no one outside the choir knew what went on there, but as long as the choir emerged Sunday by Sunday in a fairly respectable state, no questions were asked and everybody kept themselves to themselves.

On the pretence that he saw a parishioner approaching, the vicar now directed me to a moth-eaten green baize door, and dissolved into the shadows. I forged ahead alone and entered the choir vestry.

It was so dim in here that I thought I was one of those pilgrims who keep on marching through the night of doubt and sorrow. However, I soon got my bearings, and noticed that the two tombs for which Wyatt had had no use had obviously come into their own again—as seating accommodation. They stood in the middle of the floor, covered with the names of generations of sacrilegious choir-boys.

In a gallery at the back of the church

The whole of one wall was devoted to a memorial depicting two buxom ladies who leaned on an urn and looked very upset about the demise of a pious eighteenth-century pirate who lay beneath them under a two-ton slab of stone.

The remaining wall space was taken up with more heart-rending epitaphs and the usual rogue's gallery of Victorian choir outings showing large groups of villainous-looking, black-bearded, straw-hatted gentlemen standing in front of pubs. And squeezed between these, tastefully draped with cobwebs, were two framed lists—one showing the season's fixtures for the choir darts team, and the other giving the names of the choristers temporarily absent at the Boer War.

In the great tradition of church choirs everyone suddenly materialized about two minutes before the service was due to start. But these were experts. They were ready, men, boys and girls, dead on time. And so was I—kindly rigged out in a cassock and surplice which must have been still waiting for one of those members on the Boer War list.

We were accommodated round the organ in a gallery at the back of the church, so while the vicar entered the chancel dignified and alone, the choir clambered to their places up a ladder and through a trapdoor. When the hollow clumping of hobnailed boots and clatter of high heels had subsided, the vicar cast one apprehensive and despairing glance at the gallery to make sure that we were unfortunately all there, and then took no more notice of us.

I think he was trying to forget us, because he seemed to address himself entirely to the Colonel who sat with his party in the front pew. And it was quite obvious that the Colonel, despite his eighty years, was very much in charge.

For instance, this was the only church I had discovered where the congregation led the choir in the singing. As soon as a hymn was announced the Colonel would lead off his supporters with a melodious parade-ground bellow which put them well ahead of the choir, who were still finding their places. Then the organist would desperately try to overtake the choir, who would never wait for him in the futile efforts to draw level with the congregation.

To a stranger all this was a little disconcerting, but if you thought of the hymns as three part rounds it wasn't at all bad, and the *Amens* were really fascinating with their unique alpine echo effect.

The Evensong included a community hymn singing session, so we had many opportunities to beat the Colonel, but we never did. Always we arrived at the last verse a breathlessly gallant second, with the organist a bad third.

Of course the inference might be drawn that the parties concerned could not have been on very good terms, but this would be quite wrong. The Colonel had been a great sportsman in his day and had always appreciated worthy, game opponents.

SINGING IN THE RAIN

ONCE, in the days when I still had a touching faith in the existence of the English summer, I holidayed in a small village in the shadow of the White Horse hills of Berkshire.

As usual, I worked my way into the local church choir, and thus added another chapter to my appalling musical background.

The vicar, a pale and eager young man, said he was only too pleased to welcome anyone—just anyone—who was willing to have a go in the choir, no matter what kind of voice they had—as so many members were on holiday enjoying the rain somewhere else.

He explained that on this particular Sunday a special opening ceremony had been arranged for the new children's recreation ground at the rear of the church. A strong choir was needed to lead the important parish officials in the singing of three of the only six hymns which they all vaguely knew.

At 5.30 in the afternoon the choir, consisting of about twenty men, boys and girls, processed out of the vestry and through the jungle of the graveyard to the new recreation ground.

Of course, the usual fine refreshing summer deluge was doing its best, and so that we should not get too refreshed we were all grouped under an ancient oak tree with the important parish officials, while members of the public

A refreshing summer deluge was doing its best

were left high—but hardly dry—to do what they could with sunshades and newspapers.

Meanwhile the vicar took up his position on a kind of dais near the new, gaily-painted children's slide, down which the rain was cascading like a joyous mountain waterfall.

Our tree broke the force of the deluge, and only gentle streams of dirty water from the branches filtered through on most of the choir. I was on the end of the row, however, and could hardly get under the tree at all, but it didn't matter much because the branch nearest me was dead and supported no foliage anyway.

We sang the first hymn, 'All things bright and beautiful,' and then the vicar, still very eager, commenced his speech. It started very well, and I think he was hitting many nails firmly on the head, but I must admit that my attention wandered a little as I noticed the row of choirgirls in front of me growing shorter and shorter as their high heels sank deeper and deeper into the mud.

Then, as the vicar waxed more eloquent, he won my attention again. He beamed at his congregation and talked about the sunshine that their children brought into their lives. And the man next to me, his eyes fixed in glassy attention, discreetly cuffed the top choirboy who was discreetly splashing mud all over a junior choirgirl's white socks.

Finally the vicar pointed dramatically to the White Horse hills, which were completely obliterated in rain and clouds, and said how splendid it was that the village children could now play in this spot within sight of one of the most beautiful views in the British Isles.

So persuasive was he that I found myself straining my eyes in the direction of his outflung hand, but as visibility was down to a few yards all I could make out was a ramshackle tavern called 'The Artichoke,' which sprawled tipsily by the side of an evil-smelling duck pond.

The most important of the important parish officials now came forward with his wife to say his little piece, and cut a pink ribbon which was stretched across the main entrance of the ground. He was a small man who had probably been pushed into public life against his will by his wife, a very forceful and determined looking woman. Anyway his heart wasn't in this bit of public life, for he looked really very pitiful as he dejectedly declared how very happy he was to be present.

To make matters worse, he had forgotten his scissors, and there was a delay while someone untied the ribbon from the fence, while his wife regarded him in a most unfriendly way.

Finally the choir came into their own again, and the congregation cheered themselves up, with the raucous singing of two more popular hymns.

These hymns had no bearing whatsoever on the occasion and indeed even contradicted each other. But, with few exceptions, it is the composers of the tunes, not the writers of the words, which have made our English hymns famous. The average Englishman will happily sing any words to a good tune.

We now returned to the church for Evensong, and it struck me that the locals must have been quite used to the blessings of continual rain, because no one in the choir seemed in the least perturbed as we squelched into the choir stalls to open the service with 'The radiant morn has passed away.' I think they even considered the whole proceedings a little tame, for during the sermon the man next to me recalled wistfully the occasion when they had sung at the opening of the new almshouses. There had been a thunder-storm then, and the place had been struck by lightning.

After the service the vicar seemed to sense that I wasn't so keen on water as were his flock, and realizing that I was faced with a goodish walk to my lodgings, he said that we'd take a short cut to the vicarage and he'd lend me an umbrella. The short cut was twice as far as the normal way and involved negotiating a field that had turned itself into a lake.

By the time we reached the vicarage it didn't much matter whether I had an umbrella or not. However, I opened it, and at that moment the sun burst through the clouds like a huge glowing face. It grinned at me wickedly. . . .

IT'S AN ILL WIND

I PREFER the country to the seaside, but on one rare occasion I holidayed at a small but well-known South Coast resort.

Owing to circumstances beyond the control of the motor coach company—or anyone else for that matter—I arrived four and a half hours late in a state of suppressed fury. I was therefore in no mood to appreciate the bright little promenade, with its gaily painted lamp standards between which were strung dozens of coloured electric light bulbs, and behind which there seemed to be almost as many beach photographers who kept springing out on me and insisting on taking my photograph.

The place was thronged with people wearing funny paper hats which invited all and sundry to 'Kiss me quick' and 'Hold me tight,' but as I merely wanted a good meal and a night's sleep I took no notice and hurried on.

After a brief pre-arranged call on the local vicar, during which I engineered an invitation to sing in the choir the next day, I retired to my guest house.

I awoke much refreshed with a feeling that I was really going to enjoy this holiday. A terrific thunderstorm was in progress and the Sunday papers said that the weather would continue to deteriorate and that further outlook was the same.

However, the rain had eased a little as church time approached, and I again made my way along the bright little promenade. A large official noticeboard welcomed me to the sunshine and golden beaches of the town, and there followed a list of amenities designed to help me enjoy myself, but I couldn't quite make out what they were because the bottom of the board was veiled in a curtain of mud thrown up from the pavement by the force of incessant rain.

Only one man sat on the beach, tastefully attired in bathing-trunks and a trench coat with the collar turned up. But quite a large number of holidaymakers were wending their way to church. They were all trying to persuade themselves that they would have attended service even if the sun *had* been shining, and were looking very righteous as they parked their streaming umbrellas and hung their macs over the backs of pews.

I found the vicar in the vestry, but, although he had already made my acquaintance, he seemed at a loss to know who I was or what I wanted. Eventually, however, he obligingly introduced me to the organist as someone bearing a name quite unlike my own and coming from a place I'd never heard of.

I, of course, righted the matter with the organist who excused the vicar's lapse by explaining that I'd arrived at a very tricky time when he was engrossed in his usual Sunday morning pastime of changing most of the hymns at the last minute and substituting different tunes for those that remained.

When the service was about to start, the organist, who appeared to be a very cultured and well-spoken man, called the choir together to give his final instructions. He said: 'I hope to goodness you lot will at least *try* to keep the Smart in F *Te Deum* in tune this Sunday, because last week it sounded something awful!'

Would they also please remember that this week all the collections were going to the choir outing fund. If they had to depend on the regular congregation who *knew* them they naturally couldn't expect a brass farthing, but luckily

Looking very righteous

the weather had forced along a great many visitors who might be induced to give generously if only the choir's efforts were not too excruciating. It was a case of fooling most of the people *some* of the time.

He appealed to the boys, therefore, to make an all out effort to look as though they were normal and had a vague idea of what they were supposed to be doing. And would the altos who seemed to imagine they were barn-owls calling to their mates please soft pedal the hooting, and the basses remember that they were supposed to be singers and not steamrollers.

Finally—just because the service was to conclude with the singing of 'All Hail the Power' to the tune 'Diadem,' it was no excuse for the choir to imagine they were at a revivalist meeting or on a roundabout, so would they kindly refrain from going wild. Of course, the congregation would get into the usual fantastic muddle wondering whether to sing the long 'Crown Him' with the trebles and tenors, or the short sharp 'Crown Hims' with the altos and basses, but if any of the boys were caught openly laughing at them they'd cop it good and proper afterwards.

Noting the look of admiration on my face, a fellow alto beamed at me joyously. 'Terrific, isn't he?' he enthused, 'we wouldn't miss his little Sunday morning homilies for the world. He didn't mention the tenors this week but last week he called them the biggest lot of . . .' But I never heard what the tenors were. The vicar weighed in just then, and shepherded us all into the chancel.

The church was packed. I am sure everyone enjoyed the service, particularly 'All Hail the Power.' As the organist had forecast, the congregation did get mixed up with the 'Crown Hims' which came at us on all sides like pistol-shots, but such was the impact of the flamboyant Victorian tune that everyone felt impelled to sing to the last note—flat or sharp, in time or out.

The composer of 'Diadem,' James Ellor, was an obscure hatmaker and railway labourer who wrote only one tune in his life. He thought it would go no further than the tiny country chapel where he led the choir, but it went round the world and it worked a miracle—it made Church of England congregations forget themselves, forget their weather, and *sing*!

THE GREAT DIVIDE

DURING a visit to an old friend in Dorsetshire, I was much flattered by the local vicar's pressing invitation to sing in the village church choir—until my friend explained a few things to me in a most blunt and brutal manner. Apparently, owing to the freak architecture of the church, the chancel was far more spacious than the nave, and the vicar, a hearty, blundering type, had therefore always invited visitors into the choir whether they could sing or not.

By this means he not only avoided overcrowding in the pews, but had long ago reduced the organist to a brooding introvert who had given up all hope of teaching anyone to sing. Sheer force of habit was responsible for his regular appearance in the organ loft, where he crouched Sunday by Sunday assailed by the most uproarious, unrecognizable singing, and wondered why he'd ever been born.

My friend suggested that knowing the facts I might still be surprised at the size of the choir, for a few weeks ago it had more than doubled itself overnight.

It appeared that a very advanced young organist had recently been appointed to a neighbouring church, and his first action had been to call his choir together for a friendly discussion on their future musical policy. This consisted of the organist's firmly telling the choir what they were going to do, and even more firmly condemning anyone who held different views as a stick-in-the-mud or a sort of enemy of the State.

In the circumstances the friendly discussion had turned the whole choir into enemies of the State, and they had gone off to offer their allegiance elsewhere.

Their eventual invasion of the chancel of my friend's church didn't perturb the existing choir in the least, for it

A huge rubber-booted hoof

was a time-honoured tradition there that no newcomers were even noticed for the first five years, and were certainly not recognized as members of the choir until they had occupied the same choir stalls for at least double that period.

Things sorted themselves out very well on the evening of my attendance. I found myself marshalled with the enemies of the State opposite the official choir, who blandly looked through us from beneath the organ.

But, if the invaders were ignored, they fully reciprocated, for they took their singing time not from the organ but from their principal bass. He was a mountainous gentleman, looking uncannily like a wind-swept Shire horse, who kept thrusting a huge rubber-booted hoof into the chancel and drumming out a rhythm by kicking the side of the choir stall.

And the organist, brooding away in his loft, wondered with a vague excitement what on earth could possibly happen next. He soon knew!

At the appropriate spot the vicar announced the anthem and then, in the manner of vicars, settled back comfortably to check his sermon notes. It was not until the ensuing silence became oppressive that he looked up to face the fascinated gape of the whole choir, and realized that there was no anthem, and that somehow he had read from the previous Sunday's notices.

Quickly rising to the situation, he put away his sermon and gave out a hymn, but this misfired badly. It was from *A. & M.* second supplement, which was not in the books used by the congregation. The official choir had obviously never heard of it either, but it did strike a chord with some of the enemies of the State, who were stroked to victory by the rubber-booted bass, and saved the day magnificently.

The official choir recovered during the slaughtering of the next hymn, and we sang our separate ways to the point where the sermon offered some respite.

As we sat down, a choirgirl with a brazen smile and uninhibited voice handed me the parish magazine. This was an unbelievable nightmare, marked 'Price 10p. or more,' sporting a cover on which the names of every known parish official, long dead or just about alive, from the vicar to the retired grave-digger, were crammed into two square inches. No larger space was available after pride of place had been given to a photo of the church which looked as though it had been taken with a home-made camera by someone the worse for drink on a dirty night in 1890.

And it seemed that few of the parish officials had anything to say, for apart from the vicar's letter which explained that he would be away from the parish for the whole of August and half September, there was only an account of a jumble sale which raised £9.47p., and a whist drive which hadn't taken place owing to a broken gas-main outside the village hall.

The remaining space was devoted to an advertisement from a gentleman who reckoned that he could give you a dignified funeral complete with limousines at a price far cheaper than anyone else's for miles.

The sermon was now well under way. The vicar was an ex-rugger player, and managed to remind the congregation of the fact at least once a Sunday. He was preaching about Christian unity and the team spirit. My friend said he was getting at the members of the Church Council who had been at loggerheads for years over the question of replacing the lectern. Apparently he tackled some parish organization from the pulpit almost every Sunday because he could speak out fearlessly and no one could answer him back. It was, however, considered very doubtful whether the choir would ever be brought down by these tactics because they never listened to the sermon anyway.

But the vicar had planned a direct approach. Bidding me farewell after the service, he added that if I came again next year I would see a great improvement in the choir.

He had some ideas and was going to call the members together for a friendly discussion. . . .

I often wonder where the enemies of the State went after that!

THE SAUSAGE MAKER'S ORGAN

SOME time ago I spent a few days with a friend who lives in a town on the outskirts of one of our larger industrial cities. It was a very go-ahead place and progress was blatantly apparent everywhere. It was in a clean air zone, and boasted a fine new main road which cut the town completely in two, and which, if you were very alert and active, you could cross without being killed or maimed for life.

The fifteenth-century church, an architectural gem, stood in splendid isolation in the shadow of a gigantic concrete fly-over, the recent building of which had necessitated the demolishing of dozens of homes. It was, however, a very useful blot on the landscape because it allowed an almost unlimited flow of diesel lorries to pass through the town unimpeded and thus pollute the air far more thoroughly and efficiently than had been possible in the unenlightened days when the houses had stood there burning their unhealthy coal fires.

A large strip of the churchyard had also been sacrificed to accommodate the fly-over and now the traffic passed so close to the church that its homely roar filled the building continuously. Indeed it almost blotted out the screams of the low-flying jet planes which, however symbolic of thrilling progress, had always tended to be just a little distracting to devotions.

Some very backward and inconsiderate members of the congregation, who didn't seem to understand that all this was progress, and imagined that they still had the right to worship in peace, had complained bitterly. The Church Council had told them flatly that they must realize they were living in a Brave New Age, but this didn't satisfy them at all. They replied that they weren't brave enough for the Brave New Age, and anyway they wanted to hear what they were singing about on Sundays.

One of those not affected by the new conditions was the organist. In his organ-loft he lived in a world of noise, for he controlled—or tried to—one of the most out-sized organs I have ever seen.

It had been presented to the church at the turn of the century by a very generous gentleman who had made millions out of the manufacture of breakfast sausage, and who had no artistic taste whatsoever. His motto had always been 'the bigger the better' so he had ordered a five-manual instrument big and powerful enough to shatter the Royal Albert Hall.

Somehow the builders had coaxed it into the church. It bulged belligerently halfway across the chancel and overflowed into the choir vestry to such an extent that only very thin people under 5ft. 5in. could stand upright in the place. Pipes sprouted everywhere and the presence of a battered piano crammed into a corner gave the startling impression that somebody had attempted to hold a party in the engine-room of a battleship.

Some of the young people of the parish had felt very strongly about the state of the vestry, and as they couldn't remove the pipes they decided that they could at least brighten the remaining visible walls. Firmly condemning the dark Victorian décor as unworthy of the church they

We were all rather tall

brought in their do-it-yourself team with paint of every known and unknown hue.

The resulting catastrophe made it quite possible to imagine you were in an espresso coffee bar, if you turned your back on the pipes and got away from the engine-room idea.

My friend, a member of the choir, took me along to sing at Matins, and in the unique vestry introduced me to some fellow singers. We were all rather tall and stood around bent almost double, shaking hands and looking like a venerable gathering of ancient clerics.

I was told that the choir possessed some very able lady sopranos, but that I should not meet them until just before the commencement of the service. Owing to the matchbox quality of the choir vestry they robed in the parish hall at the rear of the church. This was a temporary, corrugated-iron monstrosity which had stood there for eighty-five years. For almost as long its rebuilding fund had provided a good talking point on the agenda of the church council, who hadn't the slightest intention of doing anything about it.

When the girls appeared I was entranced—with their choir caps. It has always astonished me how so many attractive fashions can be created from plain black headgear and a few hair-clips—but this set were really outstanding. The caps had been tortured and twisted into so many shapes on so many fantastic hair-styles that I almost imagined I was at a fashionable charity bazaar. It was quite comforting to note that my male colleagues stuck to the traditional parish church chorister's attire—veteran rusty cassocks discreetly held here and there with safety-pins and topped by limp, frayed, off-white surplices with broken hangers.

At eleven o'clock the vicar herded us into the chancel

to the mighty strains of the sausage-maker's organ, and I found myself shuttled to the top end of one of the magnificent black oak choir stalls. These were wonderfully carved but were not meant for relaxing in. As I sat back, an evil-looking cherub butted the back of my neck, and a creature that looked like a cross between a dragon and a certain maths mistress I once endured, kept scratching my ear.

But there was little time for relaxing, anyway. The vicar had evidently decided to fight noise with noise. Throughout the service his bellow made the usual faulty loudspeakers tremble, and spurning all quiet and gentle hymns he had introduced a selection of the most rollicking, devil-may-care revivalist tunes he could lay his hands on.

We finished with honours just about even with the traffic and jet planes, but as things are going I think they'll soon have to call in the town brass band. The church must answer the challenge of progress.

IN THE DAYS OF THY YOUTH

OUR not too serious chorister muses on the old days.

Years ago I joined my first church choir because a very revered gentleman—whom no one ever dared cross—announced to my father as we entered church one Sunday evening, 'The laddie must join the choir!'

So the next day I was a terrified probationer in a celebrated band of singers, and the choirmaster had yet another musical problem on his hands.

However, after a few months I somehow graduated from the probationers' pew under the winking gas-lamp at the back of the church to the lowest seat in the choir stalls under the unwinking eye of the choirmaster. I was now a fully-fledged member of the choir, which meant an initiation ceremony.

This was arranged entirely by the boys themselves, and consisted of being thrown into a holly bush, or over someone's wall.

In my case, at the crucial moment in the ceremony the initiation party became keenly interested in extinguishing the headlight of a veteran motor-bike parked nearby, by squeezing the tube which supplied the acetylene gas, and they nearly forgot about me. But not quite; they eventually threw me over a wall almost into the waiting jaws of the largest, most ferocious Alsatian I had ever seen.

I love all animals, but in my haste to get away from this one I kicked down an entire gate, and like the coward that

I am approached the church by a different route for weeks afterwards.

Our choirmaster was a wonderful man, and knew how to keep us in order as well as teach us to sing. His whole idea was based on a system of fines. If you made a mistake after he'd told you not to, he'd say in a fatherly voice across the top of the piano, 'You silly little boy, down you go—half-a-crown.' Of course you didn't agree with this, and if you were either brave or mad you'd try to excuse yourself. But you never got further than 'But, sir . . .' because he would then rap out, 'Answering back! Down you go again—five shillings!' So you didn't say any more.

There was, however, one chorister who never learnt. He was Irish, and insisted on saying his piece, with the result that at the end of one quarter he'd lost all his pay and owed the church tenpence.

Yet he never seemed to mind; he was an easy-going lad at heart, and just thought that the choirmaster didn't like him very much.

I have memories of many fashionable weddings in those days, when the west entrance of the church was always resplendent with scarlet canopy and carpet.

They were magnificent occasions. Everyone was superbly and correctly attired, and there always seemed to be someone's mother sobbing in the front row.

Quite understandably the same two or three hymns were used each time, and we once asked the choirmaster why we couldn't sing 'Fight the Good Fight' for a change, but he was a very happily married man and never saw the point. He merely assumed that we were even more stupid than we looked.

For two services each year we joined forces with the

Parish Church choir (ours was a daughter church). One of these occasions was the Ascension Day Evensong, which was known by us as the Annual Bawl, partly because we roared through Gounod's anthem 'Unfold ye Portals Everlasting' at the top of our voices, and partly because it gave the boys of each choir a unique opportunity to hurl insults at each other after the service.

'Remember the anthem on Sunday'

But the authorities were never foolish enough to risk a combined choir outing. Our annual 'treats' were always on different dates.

We were given a large sticky tea and taken to see the famous Lyceum pantomime. This must have been one ot the blackest days of the choirmaster's year, for apart from attempting the impossible task of keeping his villainous charges under his eye so that they shouldn't smoke in the train, he later had to listen to them ruining their voices as the principal comedian urged his audience to 'sing the chorus just once again—much louder!'

Occasionally behind the frenzied din we would hear the choirmaster's agonized voice appealing, 'That's enough, boys. Remember the anthem on Sunday.' But he knew from experience that he was wasting his breath. He remonstrated purely as a matter of principle, and would have been really surprised if anyone had taken any notice of him on that night!

But whether we could sing or merely emit horrible croaks on the following Sunday the rigid rules of cleanliness and personal tidiness were not relaxed. Voiceless or not, we were always spotless. Yet this was a miracle which will always astonish me, for the wash-basin and the mirror were the most neglected superfluities in our vestry.

Of course all that is changed now. In these enlightened days when we have those charming lady choristers to brighten and complicate our lives, every available mirror is occupied for hours. A fascinating reflection!

THE END OF THE LINE

RATHER surprisingly for these days the Somerset village where I spent a short holiday was still mercifully in the Dark Ages, boasting no new bungalow estates, new trunk roads, skyscrapers or nuclear power stations.

Following my usual custom I had got myself invited into the local church choir but was disappointed to learn that owing to the clergy shortage the church was only open Sunday morning, while Evensong was sung in the church of a neighbouring village.

However, the same choir and organist served both places, and a choirgirl who, like myself, turned out to be a railway enthusiast, suggested that we should make the evening journey by the local train which was far more interesting than the local bus, and far safer than the organist's car.

The station, which was situated in the middle of a field, was known endearingly as Grinding Halt. It was a most picturesque establishment with a booking-office containing no booking-clerk, and a waiting-room containing no seats. On the platform a large Boxer dog stood studying the time-table. Perhaps he understood it because he looked very intelligent, but to my unmathematical mind the hundreds of figures, lines, dots and pointing hands suggested nothing but a printer's nightmare.

The choirgirl understood it however, and said that it simply meant that there were three trains a day which ran whenever the engine-driver felt in the mood.

While we waited she further explained that we didn't

need tickets, as everybody paid at the other end, and that we were certain of getting there in time for the service because her brother, who was the fireman, was also the only bass in the choir, and managed to work in Evensong with his stoking.

True enough, the train soon appeared, the stout snuffling little engine looking remarkably like the Boxer dog who now abandoned the time-table and lumbered down the platform and on to the track, regarding the train with a worried frown.

The two carriages were packed solid with three regular customers, the engine-driver's bike, and about 150 railway enthusiasts from London who had heard a rumour that the line was to close and wanted to make sure of 'doing the run.'

It took a little time for the guard to ease us into the last compartment, where I had to stand with bowed head to avoid hitting the richly decorated ceiling which must have been the pride of the 1870's. Then the Boxer dog stood aside and we were on our way.

The choirgirl's brother coped splendidly with the stoking, for in no time at all we shuddered to a halt at the end of the line, which appeared to be the church graveyard. The three regular customers who were also choir members joined us, and having paid our fares to a porter who held out his hand and never looked at what we gave him, we all climbed over a wall and dodged through the tombs to the vestry.

In the vestry we came upon the organist imparting last-minute instructions about the anthem to a dangerous looking mob of choirboys who were taking no notice whatsoever.

He was an imposing figure wearing a deep frown and red carpet slippers. The choirgirl had explained that he always wore the frown owing to his contact with generations of moronic trebles. He always wore the carpet slippers also, but no one quite knew why. . . .

He seemed pleased to see me again and was, I think, about to try his last-minute anthem briefing on me, but had to excuse himself hurriedly to reprimand one of the boys who was wearing somebody else's surplice back to front.

Meanwhile a choirman handed me a yellowing sheet of paper advertising a jumble sale of ten years ago on the back of which was a spidery collection of numbers and letters. He announced briefly: 'That's what we're singing' and cuffing a boy out of his way, passed on. My choirgirl friend, who could see that I hadn't the faintest idea of how to translate the jumble into music, once again came to my rescue.

She revealed that this was the hymn list, and as it was almost unknown for the choir to use the tune set to a hymn, the hymn number was put first, followed by the initials of the hymnal. These were followed by the location of the tune. Sometimes the tune or hymn was in manuscript form and this, of course, further complicated the list. . . .

I suggested that this was all rather unusual, but she explained it away with a charming simplicity.

She said the vicar was one of those who like to show how broadminded they are by working regardlessly through almost every hymn in the book—and some outside as well. And the choir was one of those who only know about a dozen tunes which have been handed down from generation to generation, and strongly object to learning anything else. Consequently a most keen and enjoyable

Never looked at what we gave him

contest had developed between the vicar and the organist. The vicar would dig up an unknown hymn, and the organist would endeavour to fit it to one of the choir's accepted tunes. The organist and choir had never been beaten, but once they had been in grave danger of losing a point. The vicar had discovered a hymn written in such an extraordinary metre that it refused to be married off to an eligible tune.

Things looked black, and it became obvious that the choir would have to do the unthinkable and learn a new tune. However, at the last moment, the vicar was taken ill with 'flu, and a relieving priest had been prevailed upon to substitute 'Onward, Christian Soldiers.'

I remember little of the actual service except that I found a firm friend in the fireman who had got rid of his engine and sat next to me in the stalls. During the sermon we discovered that we were both fiercely *Ancient & Modern* (Standard Edition) men.

My day was made!

BOILED BEEF AND HISTORY

MY East Anglian friend always maintains that where church choirs are concerned, vicars are extremists. Either they are embarrassingly keen and are carried away with an enthusiasm which they feel entitles them to tell the choirmaster exactly how to run his choir, or else they consider the choir a necessary evil and grimly ignore it.

My friend believes that the latter attitude is often better, because if the vicar really believes he is born to direct the organist and the choir and sing every available tenor solo there is nothing much you can do about it, but if he ignores you, you can ignore him back, and practically get away with murder.

As I had sung in the village choir once or twice during holidays he considered that I was entitled to be a guest at the annual choirmen's dinner, and accordingly, one November evening, I was met from the London train by the vicar, who had kindly offered to drive me to the local tavern where the function was to be held. The vicar was very much one of the choir-ignoring type, but was always gentleman enough to endure the dinner with a good grace.

'The Sly Dog' tavern was a delightfully medieval pile all oak beams and death-watch beetle. In fact there were so many oak beams that I almost thought I was lost in a forest.

The meal was served punctually, and as soon as everybody had finished complaining about the seating arrangements and the fumes from the coke-stove, we settled down to enjoy the boiled beef.

As is often the case, conversation died until after the sweet had arrived, and then the landlord, who was also the principal bass, rose to give his well-known speech on the history of the choir. This traced its fortunes from the eighteenth century when it was merely a small band of untrained singers tucked out of sight in the gallery, to the present day when it was a much larger band of untrained singers in full view of everybody.

We followed the landlord's forbears, who had all been choir members, through the Battle of Waterloo and on to the Crimea and the Indian Mutiny. The whole thing was brought vividly to life, but for some reason, when we got to the Boer War, the landlord seemed to lose his way and we were left hopelessly floundering with his bass grandfather at Mafeking.

Fortunately, however, one of the oldest members, who had been gently snoring since we'd charged with the Light Brigade, suddenly collapsed into his lemon meringue pie. No one cared to draw his attention to this rude behaviour, but the diversion did give the organist an opportunity of butting in smartly with grateful thanks to the speaker, and calling upon someone else to cover up with 'a few words.'

This gentleman, who obviously didn't think the drinks were moving fast enough, immediately proceeded to propose a large number of toasts. They ended with one to the vicar, who didn't enjoy boiled beef and had been missed out when they brought round the lemon meringue pie.

In a charming reply he told his annual white lie about appreciating the choir, and said he often thought what a different place the church would be if they had no choir at all. Everybody cheered frenziedly at this except the man on my left who murmured 'Shame,' but I don't know whether he referred to the vicar or to a colleague opposite who had just beaten him in grabbing the last free cigarette

Collapsed into his lemon meringue pie

on the table. Anyway the vicar sat down amid the continuing applause and was soon making himself a little happier increasing the tobacco smoke, which by now had settled over the room in an uncannily good imitation of a London 'pea souper.'

The organist, who could never remember what he wanted to say and had lost the old envelope bearing his notes, now neatly by-passed his turn to speak by suggesting that some members might like to 'render something.'

Unfortunately the regular alto was working overtime owing to a 'flu epidemic at the gasworks, and I suddenly found myself part of a quartet gathered round the piano. Out of the fog someone thrust a music copy into my hands and told me I knew the piece well. I'd never heard the thing in my life, but before I could protest we were off.

To this day I have no idea what we sang. All I remember is that at the conclusion the landlord's cat, who had been sitting on the mantelpiece, threw me a look of utter contempt and walked out.

I think he was a little unfair. Granted I may have sung a shade flat, but that piano would have flattened a Covent Garden prima-donna, let alone a parish church alto.

From this point the evening wore on happily with everyone singing a solo or performing on his favourite instrument. One man who for years had played Suppé's 'Light Cavalry' on his mouth-organ, proudly varied his performance on this occasion by torturing a saw with a violin bow, and even the vicar was persuaded to murder some Gilbert and Sullivan.

Finally the Press arrived in the person of the 'local rag' reporter. Year after year he found it unnecessary to alter a single word of his account of the dinner, but of course he had always to make sure the same people *did* speak and say the same things. . . .

WEDDING BREAK

I WAS enjoying myself hugely at one of those country church fetes where everybody is expected to throw little wooden balls into non-receptive buckets and guess how many beans there are in a jam jar.

You are generally inveigled into performing these antics by a most charming maiden whose smile reduces the men, at least, into simpering idiots. Under the sweet influence they become more and more reckless in their efforts to please, and with their money, and the organ fund or the beetle-in-the-tower fund prospers exceedingly.

Naturally the hard core of the fete consists of the gay stalls where you can purchase a wide variety of things you don't want which you can then hand back for the next jumble sale.

To add to the romantic excitement of the whole thing there is often a fortune-teller at your service. She rejoices in a name like Madame Hamboni, and claims descent from a long line of fortune-tellers who foretold the fates of all the crowned heads of Europe. Actually she is a local lady who, of course, knows the business of everyone in the village from constant consultation at the local post office. Heavily disguised with cocoa and ear-rings she pretends she is learning about you for the first time as she gazes into the depths of her upturned goldfish bowl.

The lady at this fete was doing a brisk trade dispensing promises of dark lovers, unlimited travel and tons of money, and I was about to join the queue for my share when my friend with whom I was holidaying suddenly appeared and grabbed my arm.

'Come on,' he gasped, 'here's a chance to do your stuff. Our choir has got a job.' He was in a tremendous hurry, and I had the greatest difficulty in discovering what was going on as he dragged me all over the fete ground rounding up members of the church choir.

As far as I gathered, it appeared that a dreadful mistake had been made at a neighbouring church. Owing to a confusion of dates the choir and organist had gone off to a music festival at which they always won first prize, and a fashionable wedding due to take place within the hour was in danger of being left high and dry.

As a last resort their vicar had appealed for help to our choir. He knew that they never went to music festivals. They never went anywhere beyond their own church where they were well liked and understood by the congregation. For no matter how flat the congregation sang—and they had to be heard to be believed—they never sang quite as flat as the choir, and were therefore always filled with a false and pleasant pride in their vocal chords.

My friend said something about 'transport laid on' and shepherded about twenty uncomprehending choristers towards a disreputable horse-box. This was the conveyance of an out-sized Suffolk Punch horse named Theodore the Tank who had won the cart-horse derby held at the fete earlier in the afternoon. We clambered in behind him, and within a few moments were lurching on our way.

We made a brief stop at our church to collect our psalters which were differently pointed from those at the neighbouring church. In no time at all an obliging little choirboy flung them into the back of the horse-box in the same reverent manner that they had been flung about the choir stalls for the last half-century.

As I picked them up and brushed the straw from them a man who had been leaning nonchalantly on the rear end of Theodore and eating a bag of crisps, asked mildly where we were going, and I told him I thought it was to a wedding. Falling heavily against me and dropping his crisps as Theodore decided to move, he said that it would be a nice change because he was getting fed up with the fete anyway.

Discreetly spreading petrol fumes and straw along the bridal path our horse-box lumbered up to the church behind a Daimler full of delicious bridesmaids. We followed these up the red carpet at a respectable distance and were soon fitting ourselves out from the super choir's elegant collection of robes much to the disgust of a lordly verger who had obviously taken a violent dislike to choristers who smelt of horses and never went to music festivals.

The wedding itself was quite unremarkable. There was the usual nervous bridegroom waiting for the usual confident (late) bride. And there were the two families set in opposing camps on each side of the main aisle. When the bride eventually arrived on the arm of her father she looked what the press unfailingly describe as 'radiant,' and this seemed to have an effect on the still bemused choir who now appeared to realize for the first time why they were present and led her up the aisle at a smart shamble.

The picture was slightly varied at this point by one of our basses who appeared plodding solemnly up and down the choir stalls giving out our ragged psalters, and by the organist who was playing something which sounded like the Post Horn Gallop.

Whether the congregation realized we were not the famed, prize-winning choir which should have been singing I don't know, but they looked quite pleased with our elephantine efforts, and at the close of the service some even thanked us.

By this time Theodore the Tank had been taken home, and his horse-box was waiting to return us to the fete.

As we left, the official photographer was losing his temper posing the wedding party like statues round the church door. People with box cameras and unmanageable children kept getting in his way, and two old ladies were throwing confetti over everyone within reach. . . .